ALL YEAR ROUND

Winter

John Paull

Based on the Central television programmes

Macdonald Educational

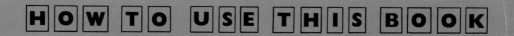
HOW TO USE THIS BOOK

First, look at the contents page opposite. The chapter list tells you what each page is about.

If you want to know about one particular thing, look it up in the index on page 30. For example, if you want to know about caves, the index tells you that there is something about them on pages 6 and 7. The index also lists the pictures in the book.

When you read this book, you will find some unusual words. The glossary on pages 28–29 explains what they mean.

Editor
Claire Llewellyn

Design
Liz Black

Production
Marguerite Fenn

Picture research
Diana Morris

Factual adviser
M G Ayres

Teacher panel
Mary Gribbin
Jules Steel

The poem on page 17 is from *Salford Road* and is included with the kind permission of the author, Gareth Owen.

Illustrations
Peter Bull: 6 (bottom), 7 (bottom), 12, 15 (bottom), 21 (top), 24
John Farman: 7 (top), 13, 20, 21 (bottom)
Robert Morton: 10, 11, 14 (top), 26
John Rignall: 8 (bottom), 9, 15 (top), 18
Kate Rogers: 6 (top), 8 (top), 17, 22 (bottom), 23, 25
Larry Ronstadt: front cover

Photographs
Ardea (P. Morris): 19 (right)
Sally & Richard Greenhill: 22 (top)
David Hosking: 19 (left)
Frank Lane Picture Agency: 16 (bottom)
Last Resort Picture Agency: 16 (top)
NHPA (Jany Sauvanet): 14
Zefa: 27

CONTENTS

H O M E S
Where do you live?

Do you think caves made good homes?

Long ago people lived in caves. They lit wood fires to keep warm and to cook their food. They slept on twigs and grass and covered themselves with animal skins. Sometimes they drew pictures on the walls. The caves were their homes.

Today people live in many different kinds of homes. But all homes have some things that are the same.

A home can be big or small, in a city, or all on its own in the country.

Our homes keep us dry and warm. They shelter us from the weather. Do you know what your home is made of? Many homes look alike from the outside, but inside they can be quite different. Like cave people, we decorate our homes. We make them comfortable and use the different rooms for different things. We prepare food in the kitchen, but we wash in the bathroom. Do you have a favourite room?

Is this the sort of house that you would like to live in?

A caravan is a special home. It is small, but there is still room to sleep, wash, cook and eat.

HOMES
Concrete jungle

Like us, other living things need a home to shelter in. Tiny animals live between stones and bricks. Plants like lichens and mosses fill the cracks and crevices in paths and walls, so chilly weather has little effect on them.

Can you find some of the small creatures that live between pavement slabs?

Walls are homes for spiders and snails.
Plants called lichens and mosses live there too.

As winter comes on, small creatures wriggle between slabs and crawl under stones. Their dark homes shelter them from the cold and wet.

Ivy, which grows on old brick walls, flowers in winter. The flowers give honey to winter moths, bees and flies. The leaves shelter snails which cluster in groups when it is cold. The snail has its own special home – its shell. When a snail sleeps, it draws up inside its shell and shelters somewhere safe. Perhaps you can find one on an old wall in your road.

When a snail goes to sleep, it seals its shell with slimy mucus. This protects the snail and keeps it dry.

Winter parks and gardens can look lifeless, but earwigs, beetles and many other tiny creatures live there.

Parks and gardens are homes, too, for hedgehogs and mice. They come out at night to look for food. If you are very quiet, you might hear a hedgehog crunching on a snail. You could try leaving out some bread and milk. It may be gone in the morning!

After rain, when the earth is soft, or after snow, you may find tracks on the ground. What sort of print does a cat leave? What do bird tracks look like?

A visiting hedgehog may leave clues: tracks, broken snail shells or droppings.

Rabbit tracks show their large feet. Their droppings are small and round.

Rabbits dig underground homes called warrens. Several families live together in each warren. Badgers, too, live as families underground. Their homes are called sets. Badgers are nocturnal animals and come out at dusk to search for worms, beetles and berries.

Badgers like to eat grubs in old trees. Look for claw marks, tracks or droppings.

Sometimes it gets so cold that houses, roads and fields get covered with ice. Inside our homes though, it is warm and dry. Homes are heated by gas, electricity, wood, coal, oil or the sun's energy. How is your home heated? Fuel is expensive so we 'dress' our homes so heat is not wasted. This is called insulation.

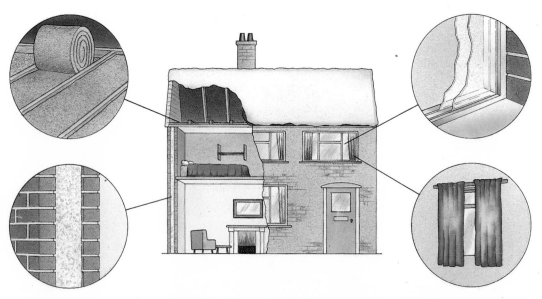

We double-glaze windows, fill up the gaps between walls, line the attic floor and hang curtains to keep the warmth in. How is your home insulated?

Human beings need to keep warm. Food is like a fuel for us. It keeps us warm and it gives us energy to do all the things we want to do. We ought to eat a good breakfast to keep healthy.

How do you keep warm when you go to school on cold days? Which are your warmest clothes? A coat, gloves, a scarf and a hat stop heat from leaving the skin.

TO SCHOOL

COLD DAYS
Out in the cold

Pond grasses look dead in winter, but their underground roots will grow again in the spring.

Cold birds fluff out their feathers and trap warm air.

Dressed in your warmest clothes, it's fun to go walking on a frosty morning. Grass and plants are white with frost. There doesn't seem to be much life around. But if you look inside the dry and brittle plant stems, you may see some small creatures. They will sleep until the spring.

In cold weather, birds need plenty of food to keep warm and healthy. When there is snow on the ground, birds cannot find all the food they need. You could leave scraps out for them or put up a bird table at school or in the garden. Make sure that cats can't reach it.

Some birds eat insects or berries. Others will visit your table. Which birds are they? What do they eat?

Birds like to eat bread, but it mustn't be mouldy. They like bacon rind, seeds, nuts and a drink of water. How many different birds visit your table? What do they like to eat? Remember: once you start to feed your birds, you must do it every day. They rely on you.

We saw these birds today

Bluetit	🐦🐦🐦🐦
row	🐦🐦
inch	🐦
cird	

What the birds ate

	Chaffinch Sparrow Bluetit
	Sparrow Bluetit
	Blackbird
	Thrush

COLD DAYS
Surviving the winter

Winter is a quiet time when many living things rest. Some creatures live inside our homes, sharing our warmth and food, tucked away in corners. Can you find spiders in your home? Windows and ceilings are good places to look.

Cats grow lazy in winter and snooze in the warm.

Cats live with us inside our homes. They find the warmest spots and spend most of each day sleeping. They grow thicker coats, too. Squirrels have a thick fur coat and stay in their homes during the very cold weather, feeding on their stores of nuts. Their homes are called dreys.

Squirrels line their dreys with leaves and twigs.

Winter days

Biting air
Winds blow
City streets
Under snow

Noses red
Lips sore
Runny eyes
Hands raw

Chimneys smoke
Cars crawl
Piled snow
On garden wall

Slush in gutters
Ice in lanes
Frosty patterns
On window panes

Morning call
Lift up head
Nipped by winter
Stay in bed

Gareth Owen

RESTING
A winter rest

In winter many living things slow down and sleep. Insects rest in cracks and crevices, in rotting logs or under rocks.

If you carefully lift up a flat rock you will see lots of tiny creatures resting. Millipedes and centipedes curl up when they are cold and remain still. They try to save their body heat. Can you find one? If you can, pick one up, hold it in your hand and watch. What happens? Put the creature back carefully. What happens when you do that? Put the rock back slowly and carefully. It is home for lots of creatures.

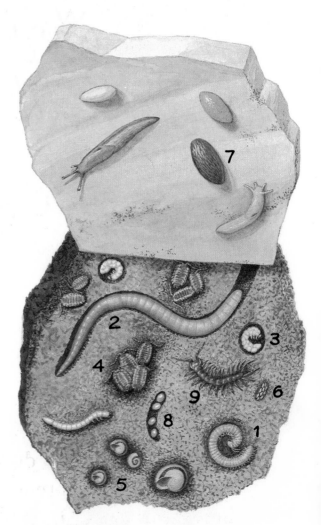

Under a rock, look for:

1 Millipede	5 Banded snails
2 Earthworm	6 Spider eggs
3 Beetle larvae	7 Slugs
4 Woodlice	8 Snail eggs
9 Centipede	

The toad eats as much as it can before hibernation. It then lives off its body fat.

The dormouse hibernates in a warm place, protecting itself from the cold.

You might be lucky and see a toad under your rock. They go into a deep sleep in the winter. This is called hibernation. The animal hardly breathes, goes quite cold and lives off its body fat. Dormice hibernate in nests made of fur and leaves. They curl up in a ball so they do not lose as much body heat. Leave any animal if it is hibernating. Don't try to wake it up.

RESTING
The family at rest

You need to rest your mind as well as your body.

Rest keeps us healthy and alert. We need to rest our minds and our bodies every day. After a hard day's work at home, in the factory, the office or school, people rest in different ways. How do you like to rest after a busy day? What about the other members of your family?

Most people take a little rest when they are working hard. They may stop for a drink or a chat, or they may want to stretch their legs. Do you sometimes rest your eyes when you are reading or watching television?

At the end of the day we rest by sleeping. Everybody needs a good night's rest, but some people need more sleep than others. What time do you go to bed? What time do you wake up? See if you can find out how long the other people in your house sleep.

Children often go to bed before grown-ups because they need more sleep. Do you think you need more sleep than a grown-up? What sorts of things make you tired?

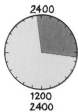
Mum sleeps 7 hours every night.

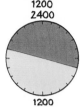
I am 6 years old. I sleep 12 hours every night.

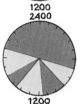
Baby Tom sleeps all night and has 2 naps in the day.

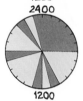
Our dog Spot sleeps all night and during the day.

While children sleep, Mum and Dad can rest or get on with work around the home.

RESTING
Fast and slow

You need to rest your body after exercise. This is one reason why some sports have a half-time break.

When we exercise, our heart beats faster. You can count your heart beat. It is called the pulse rate. Find a friend's pulse inside the wrist. Count the number of beats in a minute. Now ask your friend to run on the spot for two minutes. Count the pulse again. How many beats are there now?

Use your first and second fingers to find the pulse on the inside of your wrist.

Exercise makes our muscles work hard and they need more oxygen from the air we breathe in. What happens to your breathing when you are moving fast? Check this by carrying out an experiment.

Count the breaths you take in a minute when you are at rest. Then exercise for two minutes. Now count the breaths you take in a minute again. Is there a big difference between the two counts?

Name	Breathing rate	
	Before exercise	After exercise
Robert	25	28
Aziz	24	26
Ratna	23	26
Rachel	24	27

BREATHING
All living things breathe

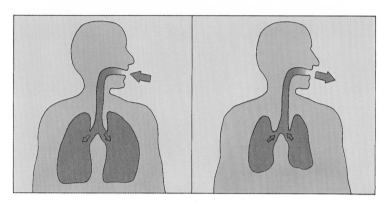

We breathe in air through the nose and mouth. The air enters the two lungs.

The lungs take oxygen out of the air. We breathe out the waste and unwanted air.

All animals and plants breathe. People cannot live for more than two minutes without breathing air. Air is a mixture of different gases. The one we need to keep us alive is called oxygen. When you breathe in, air goes through your nose and down your windpipe into your lungs.

Bubbles you blow through a straw are filled with waste air from your lungs.

Who has the deepest breath in your class? How
many breaths does it take to fill a balloon?

Your lungs are like two elastic bags. They can
grow bigger or smaller. They grow bigger when
we breathe in air. They grow smaller when
we breathe out the air our body doesn't need.

Your lungs take oxygen out of the air and pass
it on to your blood, which carries the oxygen
all round your body to where it is needed.
Your body uses up oxygen to get energy from
food. This is like a very slow sort of burning. It
makes a gas called carbon dioxide. When you
breathe out, there is a lot of carbon dioxide in
your breath.

BREATHING
Breathing under water

Human beings breathe in oxygen from the air. We cannot breathe in water, and need to take a supply of air in tanks on our backs. Whales and seals need air, too. Some seals make holes in ice to get the air they need. When whales come to the surface, they breathe out waste air in a spout.

Whales and seals can hold their breath under water for a very long time.

(Opposite) Divers carry a supply of air in tanks.

GLOSSARY

beetle	An insect with a hard black body. It has wings.
carbon dioxide	A gas found in air, which has no colour, taste or smell. It is produced by us when we breathe.
centipede	A small creature with a long, thin body and many pairs of legs.
energy	When we have energy we are full of life and can do a lot of work.
fuel	Something we can burn to produce heat; food is a fuel for our body.
gas	A substance which is not solid or liquid, like air.
hibernation	A long, deep sleep during the winter.

moss	A small, flat, green or yellow plant that grows in a wet place.
mouldy	When food is mouldy, it is covered with a soft woolly growth.
mucus	A slippery liquid which is made in certain parts of an animal's body.
muscles	Muscles make our body move. They are attached to our bones.
nocturnal	A nocturnal animal gets up at night and rests during the day.
oxygen	A gas found in air, which has no colour, taste or smell. We need it to live.
pulse	The regular beat of the heart which we can feel on our wrist.

INDEX

The **dark** numbers show you where there is a picture of the subject.